Show Us
YOUR
Glory

DESTINY IMAGE BOOKS BY ROBERT HENDERSON

Issuing Divine Restraining Orders from Courts of Heaven
(with Dr. Francis Myles)

Redeeming Your Bloodline
(with Hrvoje Sirovina)

The Cloud of Witnesses in the Courts of Heaven

Prayers and Declarations that Open the Courts of Heaven

The Trading Floors of Heaven
(with Beverley Watkins)

Accessing the Courts of Heaven

Receiving Healing from the Courts of Heaven,
Curriculum

Unlocking Destinies from the Courts of Heaven,
Curriculum

Operating in the Courts of Heaven

Praying for the Prophetic Destiny of the United States and the Presidency of Donald J. Trump from the Courts of Heaven

Father, Friend, and Judge

Show Us
YOUR
Glory

THE PRAYER THAT
OPENS NEW DIMENSIONS
OF SUPERNATURAL ENCOUNTER

ROBERT
HENDERSON

DESTINY IMAGE® PUBLISHERS, INC.

P.O. Box 310, Shippensburg, PA 17257-0310

"Promoting Inspired Lives."

This book and all other Destiny Image and Destiny Image Fiction books are available at Christian bookstores and distributors worldwide.

Cover design by Eileen Rockwell
Interior design by Terry Clifton

For more information on foreign distributors, call 717-532-3040.

Reach us on the Internet: www.destinyimage.com.

ISBN 13 TP: 978-0-7684-5359-1
ISBN 13 eBook: 978-0-7684-5360-7

For Worldwide Distribution, Printed in the U.S.A.
1 2 3 4 5 6 7 8 / 24 23 22 21 20

CONTENTS

CHAPTER 1

GLORY: THE PURSUIT OF THE GODLY

When I think of the glory of God, I think of that which the holy people of God long for. We are actually created for this glory. There is an awareness in us that His glory is what we yearn for. We were actually created to partake of His glory in a right order. I am aware that the Lord said in Isaiah 42:8 that His glory He wouldn't allow to be shared with another.

> *I am the Lord, that is My name;*
> *And My glory I will not give*
> *to another,*
> *Nor My praise to carved images.*

This statement is not about us as His people experiencing the glory and intense presence of the Lord. This verse is speaking of who *gets the glory* for what God has done. This is what God said He would not share. Whoever gets the glory is the one people will look too. Only God can fill and meet the needs of people. If someone else get the glory for what God has done, then there will be a misdirection of trust and faith. People will hope in something or someone who cannot meet their cry. This is why God says He will not allow a person, idol, or anything else to get the credit. It would cause people to look in the wrong direction and put their faith in that which cannot deliver.

However, we are allowed by God and strongly urged to seek after His glory. Second Corinthians 5:4-5 lets us know that this is what we are yearning for. Whether people know it or not, the glory of God is what will meet the deepest longings and urges of their life. There is an internal cry and even groaning that desires to partake of and be in this glory.

> *For we who are in this tent groan,*
> *being burdened, not because we*

want to be unclothed, but further clothed, that mortality may be swallowed up by life. Now He who has prepared us for this very thing is God, who also has given us the Spirit as a guarantee.

Paul explains that while we are alive in this body we are limited by *how much* glory we can experience. For us to experience the utmost realm of God's glory and presence, we would need to have a new or resurrected body. These human/fallen bodies are no longer suitable to carry the glory of God in its extreme measures. Notice, however, that we are *prepared* for mortality to be swallowed up with immortality. Until that day when we will be able to carry the glory of God in a fuller extent, we have a portion of the Holy Spirit that is our guarantee. This means that the Holy Spirit we presently have as our Companion, Helper, and the One who anoints us with glory is only a small piece of the glory we will have.

As a result of us being prepared and created for the greater weight of glory, we are groaning for this to be reality. The present ministry of the Holy Spirit is the assurance of greater things to come. This is quite amazing given some of the weightiness that people have experienced through the Holy Spirit. Charles Finney, for example, the great revivalist, actually speaks of his encounter with the Holy Spirit.

> No words can express the wonderful love that was shed abroad in my heart. I wept aloud with

joy and love; and I do not know but I should say, I literally bellowed out the unutterable gushings of my heart. The waves came over me, and over me, one after the other, until I recollect I cried out, "I shall die if these waves continue to pass over me." I said, "Lord, I cannot bear any more"; yet I had no fear of death.

Finney in his mortality struggled to carry the weight of glory that the Holy Spirit brought into his life. If the glory of God is this powerful through the Person of the Holy Spirit, as the guarantee, then what would the full manifestation of God be like? Paul actually describes a little of this to Timothy in First Timothy 6:15-16. He speaks of *light* that is so intense that one cannot approach it.

> *Which He will manifest in His own time, He who is the blessed and only Potentate, the King of kings and Lord of lords, who alone has immortality, dwelling in unapproachable light, whom no man has seen or can see, to whom be honor and everlasting power. Amen.*

This is the glory that surrounds the Lord and His Throne. Paul says no man has seen or can see this. To see this One means you would die. Our fleshly bodies cannot be sustained in such glory. This is what God told Moses when he asked to see His glory. He was told that no one could see His face

and live. Exodus 33:20 lets us know that seeing the face of God is impossible for those
of us in mortal flesh.

> *But He said, "You cannot see My*
> *face; for no man shall see Me,*
> *and live."*

The glory of God carries such extreme
intensity that it would consume us. This is
probably what scripture means when we are
told God is a consuming fire in Hebrews
12:28-29.

> *Therefore, since we are receiving a*
> *kingdom which cannot be shaken,*
> *let us have grace, by which we*
> *may serve God acceptably with*
> *reverence and godly fear. For our*
> *God is a consuming fire.*

As a result of the great power of His presence and glory, we should ask for grace to serve Him with. We are incapable of serving God acceptably without His grace in our lives. It is His grace in us and through us that allows us to partake of the intensity of His glory and still be standing. As Finney said, *it was a wonderful love filled with joy.* Yet the strength of it was so tremendous that it would wash away all that was unacceptable before the Lord. What an indescribable place with the Lord. His kindness and goodness are so extreme that we are changed into His image by the hands of a loving God. May we yearn for and experience greater and greater realms of His glory and power.

CHAPTER 2

GLORY TO GLORY

We are promised in the Word of God that we can go from glory to glory in our experience in the Lord. Second Corinthians 3:18 lets us know that the changing power of God in our lives is a result of God's ever-increasing glory.

But we all, with unveiled face, beholding as in a mirror the glory of the Lord, are being transformed into the same image from glory to glory, just as by the Spirit of the Lord.

When we come before the Lord, hiding nothing, He allows us to behold His glory. This means that we in the Spirit encounter Him. The resulting effect is that His presence and revelation of who He is transforms us progressively into His very image and likeness. My experience lets me know that I am allowed a certain touch of His glory that expands His image in me. As I walk in this place, I can have an even greater touch of His glory, which produces a new likeness of Him. It is very similar to the River that

Ezekiel saw in Ezekiel 47:3-5. New and dif-
ferent measurements were set in place that
were *deeper places* each time.

> *And when the man went out to*
> *the east with the line in his hand,*
> *he measured one thousand cubits,*
> *and he brought me through the*
> *waters; the water came up to*
> *my ankles. Again he measured*
> *one thousand and brought me*
> *through the waters; the water*
> *came up to my knees. Again he*
> *measured one thousand and*
> *brought me through; the water*
> *came up to my waist. Again he*
> *measured one thousand, and it*
> *was a river that I could not cross;*
> *for the water was too deep, water*

in which one must swim, a river
that could not be crossed.

This *man* was measuring out increments of a thousand cubits. Each time, the prophet was brought through the measurement. There was water ankle deep, then knee deep, then waist deep, then waters to swim in. This is clearly emphasizing that God would measure out for us new depths of His glory for us to experience. It is interesting that each measurement required the prophet to be *brought through the waters.* This would mean that the effects of the certain measurement had to be accomplished. This is what the glory of God does. Each time we are afforded a new realm of glory, we move through it and function in it. This will ultimately change us into His image. It is impossible to be touched by His glory and not change. When we approach Him with nothing hidden, the intensity of His glory changes us.

This is what happened to Moses in Exodus 33. Moses is at first asking that the Presence of God would go with him. Exodus 33:13-14 shows Moses requesting this presence of God to go with him and not just an angel.

> *"Now therefore, I pray, if I have found grace in Your sight, show me now Your way, that I may know You and that I may find grace in Your sight. And consider that this nation is Your people."*
>
> *And He said, "My Presence will go with you, and I will give you rest."*

God agrees to send His presence with them. As this request is granted, Moses then asked for something even greater. He asked to see the glory of God. Exodus 33:18-19 reveals this cry coming from Moses.

> *And he said, "Please, show me Your glory."*
> *Then He said, "I will make all My goodness pass before you, and I will proclaim the name of the Lord before you. I will be gracious to whom I will be gracious, and I will have compassion on whom I will have compassion."*

After the Lord agrees to send His Presence, Moses then asks for His glory. This was Moses desiring to go from glory to glory. The Presence of the Lord is one thing. The glory of God is another realm. I would call the *glory realm* the intensified Presence of the Lord. The Presence of the Lord is that which accompanies us as believers. It is His closeness that affirms us and grants us confidence and assurance. This was the Presence that set the nation of Israel apart from other people. Deuteronomy 4:7 speaks of how close God was to Israel and as a result He heard their cry.

> *For what great nation is there that has God so near to it, as the Lord our God is to us, for whatever reason we may call upon Him?*

His Presence with them gave them a confidence to request and ask of Him and get answers. His Presence also produced a *rest*. God promised Moses that His Presence would go with them and He would give them this rest. This means they would have a boldness to believe that He would fight for them and stand with them in any and every conflict and need. They could be confident that they were not alone. The very Presence of God would be close to them. These and many other things are attributes of having God close. However, Moses asked for the glory. This was a next-level place of His Presence and nearness. Once someone has tasted the Presence of the Lord, it will make them yearn for the next places. This is what Moses desired. God promised him that He would allow him to see His glory.

Seeking to define the glory of God can be a difficult task. The word *glory* actually means "the weightiness of God." In the Hebrew language it is the word *kabowd*. Years ago, I had a dream where I was in my office. I stepped outside the door of my office and there was a cloud that was in the hallway. I was knocked to the floor and remember the weight of the cloud pushing down on me. I could not get up in the dream. I remember crawling under the weight of this glory. In the dream it was quite amazing. Years later the *glory cloud* actually did show up in the church. During this time phenomenal healings and other breakthroughs began to happen. As I looked back on this, I realized that what triggered it was me stepping out of my *pastoral office* and into an *apostolic function.* This was essential to functioning in the glory of the Lord. We had known the Presence of the Lord, but God then allowed us to know His glory. The result was greater manifestations of His supernatural as we hosted and entertained the weightiness of who He is.

When Moses asked to *see the glory of God,* the Lord declared that there were five things that were associated with the glory. The Lord told Moses *My goodness* will pass before you. He said He would reveal the *name of the Lord.* He said He would be *gracious* to whom He would be *gracious.* He declared He would have *compassion* on whom He would have *compassion.* He implied that out of the glory Moses would find *direction and guidance.*

These five dimensions of God are part of His glory. His goodness, graciousness, name, compassion, and direction all stem from and are a piece of the glory of God as He is revealed. This is not all that the glory of God is, but this is what God told Moses He would unveil for him as His glory passed by. We will look at each of these in the next five chapters. They will give us at least a glimpse into what we can expect as we see the glory of God.

CHAPTER 3

THE GOODNESS OF GOD

As we pursued the glory of God, which by the way is essential to actually experiencing Him in this way, I learned some valuable lessons. Our pursuit helped us get focused on what brought the majesty and glory of God into the midst of

the people. I discovered that preaching the
right things is essential to experiencing and
witnessing God's glory. We see this in the
temple that Solomon built. When the temple was finished and the dedication was
underway, as they proclaimed the goodness of God, the glory of God came. Second
Chronicles 5:13-14 shows the cloud of glory
filling this temple as there was a proclama-
tion of the goodness and mercy of God.

> *Indeed it came to pass, when the
> trumpeters and singers were as
> one, to make one sound to be
> heard in praising and thanking
> the Lord, and when they lifted up
> their voice with the trumpets and
> cymbals and instruments of music,
> and praised the Lord, saying:*

"For He is good,

For His mercy endures forever,"

that the house, the house of the

Lord, was filled with a cloud, so

that the priests could not continue

ministering because of the cloud;

for the glory of the Lord filled the

house of God.

The unified declaration of the goodness and mercy of the Lord caused the cloud of His glory to fill the temple that had been erected. The priests couldn't even fulfill their duties because of the weight of this cloud. If we are to see the glory of God manifest, we must preach and proclaim His goodness. This is because the goodness of God is the glory of God. God told Moses He would *make His goodness pass before him*. Moses would witness and be over-whelmed with the goodness of who God is.

One of the main things we need in the church today is the revelation of how good God is. His goodness is amazing. This is one of the main things Jesus came to do. He wanted to unentangle the minds of people and the way they perceived God. Therefore, Jesus displayed kindness to the people in unparalleled ways. He then proclaimed in John 14:9 that in seeing Jesus they had seen the Father.

> *Jesus said to him, "Have I been with you so long, and yet you have not known Me, Philip? He who has seen Me has seen the Father; so how can you say, 'Show us the Father'?"*

As Jesus lived His life on the earth and brought good to all who came to Him, He was displaying the very character, nature, and heart of God the Father. Jesus came to give the world another view of who God is. He is our loving, caring Father who gives us what we could never deserve. His love for us is unmatched and His goodness is unwarranted, yet He grants us this and so much more. As the glory of the Lord appears, we begin to partake of this goodness that Jesus came to reveal.

Throughout Jesus' teaching and ministry these aspects of God were revealed. We can see this is the teaching in Matthew 20:1-16, where Jesus tells the story of the man hiring laborers for his vineyard. The master of the vineyard in this story hires these laborers throughout the day. Some are hired at the beginning of the day. Others are hired throughout the process of the day. There are even those hired at the end of the day for only one hour's work. When it is time to be paid, they each get a day's wage for their labors. Those who worked all day began to complain against the owner of the vineyard. The owner points out, however, that they had *agreed* with him for their wage. The other workers had labored on the basis of *whatever is right*. Let's look at this story.

> *For the kingdom of heaven is like a landowner who went out early in the morning to hire laborers for his vineyard. Now when he had agreed with the laborers for a denarius a day, he sent*

them into his vineyard. And he went out about the third hour and saw others standing idle in the marketplace, and said to them, "You also go into the vineyard, and whatever is right I will give you." So they went. Again he went out about the sixth and the ninth hour, and did likewise. And about the eleventh hour he went out and found others standing idle, and said to them, "Why have you been standing here idle all day?" They said to him, "Because no one hired us." He said to them, "You also go into the vineyard, and whatever is right you will receive."

So when evening had come, the owner of the vineyard said to his steward, "Call the laborers and give them their wages, beginning with the last to the first." And when those came who were hired about the eleventh hour, they each received a denarius. But when the first came, they supposed that they would receive more; and they likewise received each a denarius. And when they had received it, they complained against the landowner, saying, "These last men have worked only one hour, and you made them equal to us who have borne the burden and the heat of the day." But he answered one of them and said, "Friend, I am doing you no wrong. Did you not agree with me for a denarius? Take what is yours and go your way. I wish to give to this last man the same as to you. Is it not lawful for me to do what I wish with my own things? Or is your eye evil because I am good?" So the last will be first, and the first last. For many are called, but few chosen.

The *first* group that *agreed* were the Jews. Jesus was sent first to the lost sheep of Israel. They had an agreement with God called the *law.* They served God from this perspective. However, every other group that went to work in the vineyard went on the basis of grace. They trusted the generosity, liberality, goodness, and kindness of the owner. They did not agree on what their pay would be but simply knew the owner would do right. The result was they received a greater reward and pay than those who worked all day. Jesus was seeking to show that things were transitioning from the law to grace. There can still be a serving God from a legalistic place. However, if we can see the goodness of God and who He is revealed in Jesus, we can transition into serving the Lord from grace. The result will be a greater blessing and results that come from this place. Jesus came to help us see how good God really is. The revelation of His goodness is a part of His glory. May we behold Him and be amazed at the goodness of who He really is.

CHAPTER 4

THE NAME OF THE LORD

As Moses requested to see the glory of the Lord, God promised to put him in a cleft of the rock and pass before him. The Lord said in response to Moses' cry to see His glory that He would, *"Proclaim the Name of the Lord."* The revelation of the

Name of the Lord therefore is a part of the glory of the Lord. When we speak of the *Name of the Lord,* we are talking about the nature, character, and personhood of God. We are speaking of who He is and the way He does things. When we know God and do not just know about Him, we have made a major transition. This is why Paul's cry was to *know Him.* Philippians 3:10-11 unveils this cry that Paul as a seasoned apostle still had yearning from deep inside.

> *That I may know Him and the power of His resurrection, and the fellowship of His sufferings, being conformed to His death, if, by any means, I may attain to the resurrection from the dead.*

Paul wanted to *know him*. He wanted to know the power associated with His resurrection. He also wanted to *know* the closeness of who He is in suffering and to even be conformed to His death. In other words, that Paul would die to his own desires and activities and be a full reflection of who Jesus in in the flesh. Paul longed to know the Lord in every place and dimension. Notice that Paul connects knowing the Lord in this level to partaking of His resurrection life and power. It is in knowing Him that we have life. This is according to John 17:3.

> *And this is eternal life, that they may know You, the only true God, and Jesus Christ whom You have sent.*

Real life that is His resurrected life is a result of knowing the Lord. When we know Him, it is because the Name of the Lord is being revealed to us. We are learning His character, nature, integrity, trustworthiness, and ways. This is what we spend our years here on earth doing and also all eternity. The Lord we serve is past finding out, we are told in Romans 11:33.

> *Oh, the depth of the riches both of the wisdom and knowledge of God! How unsearchable are His judgments and His ways past finding out!*

His ways being *past finding out* simply means that we can never totally and completely come to the full understanding of who God is. There will always be

another dimension of Him to discover. He
is without explanation. There are things
we do learn of and come to know of Him.
However, there will always be other mys-
teries of Him to see and know. This is why
God told Moses He would *Proclaim the
Name of the Lord* before him. He would
allow him to see dimensions of Him that
had been withheld until this point. This is
seeing His glory. Paul actually said that as
New Testament believers, we *learn of Him*
in Ephesians 4:19-23.

> *Who, being past feeling, have
> given themselves over to lewd-
> ness, to work all uncleanness
> with greediness. But you have not
> so learned Christ, if indeed you
> have heard Him and have been*

*taught by Him, as the truth is in
Jesus: that you put off, concerning
your former conduct, the old man
which grows corrupt according to
the deceitful lusts, and be renewed
in the spirit of your mind.*

Paul speaks of those who have given
themselves over to the lust of the flesh. They
are now dominated by their own appe-
tites and cravings that lead to great sinful
activity. He then declares, *but you haven't
learned Christ.* In other words, you realize
this is not compatible with who Jesus is. You
know that living this way is not to be associated with being a believer. Therefore, we
are to deal with these desires, longings, and
compulsions with great seriousness. We are
to put them away, and in their place let our

minds be renewed with what we know and understand of Jesus as our Lord!

However, this all flows out of what we have come to know of *Christ*—who God really is. This would be a result of us having witnessed and partaken of the glory of God. We would have been impacted by the Lord Himself, proclaiming the Name of the Lord and the revelation of Him into our lives. This will cause a radical shifting of the way we live. People who claim to have had encounters with His glory and yet seem to be able to live unholy lives with no regret or remorse are a mystery. This would seem completely impossible from scripture. The glory of God revealed to us will propel us to new places of purity. It will require that we put away sinful activities and be changed from the inside out.

This is no big task, because His glory actually produces this. When we see Him in His glory, our nature is changed. We are renewed in the spirit of our minds. What used to captivate our thoughts, those powers are now broken. They are replaced with a hunger and desire for His godliness in us. This is a result of the Lord proclaiming His Name to us and us learning of Christ. The more we see Him in His glory, the more we will be compelled to be like Him. It is a process we all go through and will go through until we see Him face to face. This is actually one of the ultimate purposes of God. We are being changed into the image of the One who loved us and gave Himself for us.

Romans 8:29 tells us this was the intent of God from the beginning.

> *For whom He foreknew, He also predestined to be conformed to the image of His Son, that He might be the firstborn among many brethren.*

The Lord desires a race of people who are in the very image and likeness of His Son. He desires many who reflect this nature. As He unveils His Name to us, the glory associated with it does this work. Thank the Lord for not only calling us to holiness but also producing it in us through His glory. He who started the good work in us will also finish and complete it as we behold His glory and respond to Him.

CHAPTER 5

THE GRACIOUSNESS OF GOD

As the Lord set Moses inside the cleft of the rock, He told Him He would be *gracious to whom He would be gracious*. The glory of God is a display of the grace of God at work. Any encounter with the glory of

God will always involve God's grace. Many think that grace is only a New Testament idea. The scripture does say in John 1:17 that Jesus' coming into the earth did begin an era of grace.

> *For the law was given through Moses, but grace and truth came through Jesus Christ.*

The dispensation of the law that came under Moses was changing to a time of grace and truth that Jesus was ushering in. However, this does not mean that grace was not a part of the very character and nature of God in the Old Testament. People who think God had a sudden change to who He is when the New Testament era came are wrong. God has always been gracious. It was the activity of Jesus that allowed this nature of God to be revealed. We see the Lord being proclaimed to be gracious in many places. One of them is Psalm 116:5.

> *Gracious is the Lord, and*
> *righteous;*
> *Yes, our God is merciful.*

The word *gracious* comes from the Greek word *chanan.* It means to bend or stoop in kindness to an inferior. This is a great understanding and description of grace. The grace that Jesus brought comes from the gracious character of God that bends and stoops to us who are inferior. Psalm 113:5-9 gives this idea to us. It speaks of the kindness of God that will reach to us in our burned out and even destroyed lives. As He extends Himself and we respond, we can be lifted to places of great life, power, influence, enjoyment, and blessings.

> *Who is like the Lord our God,*
> *Who dwells on high,*
> *Who humbles Himself to behold*
> *The things that are in the heavens*
> *and in the earth?*
> *He raises the poor out of the dust,*
> *And lifts the needy out of the*
> *ash heap,*
> *That He may seat him*
> *with princes—*
> *With the princes of His people.*
> *He grants the barren woman*
> *a home,*
> *Like a joyful mother of children.*
> *Praise the Lord!*

Even though the Lord dwells in the highest place, He humbles Himself to behold us in our low position. He doesn't stop there, however. He reaches to us and lifts us up. The poor are lifted out of the dust. This speaks of the struggle in the nitty gritty of life. The mundane fight to not just overcome but to survive. God reaches to us in His graciousness and lifts us up. He also lifts us from the ash heap. Of course, anything that is ashes is something that has been burned up. Many people find themselves in a burned-out place. Their lives are destroyed and everything has been lost. All that is left are ashes. God in His grace lifts these up and gives them a position among leaders. He seats these with the princes and influential people. What a drastic demonstration and idea of grace. He also grants the barren children and a home. Those who are unfruitful, frustrated, and perhaps held in bitterness find their deepest longing fulfilled. This is the result of the gracious nature of who God is. This is a result of His glory. We began to see and experience the grace of God in our lives. Destructive places are redeemed. Terrible circumstances are turned around. What at one time would have seemed unrecoverable is restored to a dimension not considered or thought about. This is His grace flowing from His gracious life.

This is what Jesus brought to us. In fact, everything I have described is what Jesus did. Even though He is God, He laid this aside to *stoop or come down* to us. Philippians 2:6-11 shows us the willingness of Jesus as

God to bend Himself and behold what was in the earth. He also stooped and came down to us to bring us His grace. He not only brought the grace but manifested His nature that flows from His graciousness.

> *Who, being in the form of God, did not consider it robbery to be equal with God, but made Himself of no reputation, taking the form of a bondservant, and coming in the likeness of men. And being found in appearance as a man, He humbled Himself and became obedient to the point of death, even the death of the cross. Therefore God also has highly exalted Him and given Him the name which is above*

every name, that at the name
of Jesus every knee should bow,
of those in heaven, and of those
on earth, and of those under the
earth, and that every tongue
should confess that Jesus Christ
is Lord, to the glory of God the
Father (Philippians 2:6–11).

He came as a mortal man. As a mortal man He humbled Himself. He humbled Himself to death. Yet not just any death but the cruelest of deaths—the cross. This scripture alone demonstrates four distinct ways that Jesus manifested grace toward us. He became a mortal man, humbled Himself even further when found in this state, He died in this humility, yet also on the cross. Each of these represent the graciousness of

God toward us. This is the grace that God reveals in His glory. As we behold the glory of who He is, we experience the grace of God within that glory. May we encounter Him in His majesty and always see His beauty.

CHAPTER 6

THE COMPASSION OF THE LORD

As the Lord agreed to show Moses His glory, He told him He would *have compassion on whom He would have compassion.* This word *compassion* in the Hebrew is *racham*. It means *to love and be compassionate.* It actually means *to fondle.* So the idea is the loving touch of God on our lives. Compassion is the very thing that moves the Lord toward us. As Jesus walked the earth there were several times when He was moved by compassion. Matthew 9:36 says Jesus was moved with compassion because the people didn't have a shepherd.

> *But when He saw the multitudes, He was moved with compassion for them, because they were weary and scattered, like sheep having no shepherd.*

The people, as sheep, were weary and scattered because there was no one to pastor them. This moved the heart of Jesus. He understood that there were certain needs that only a shepherd/pastor could meet. A miracle couldn't fix the problem.

A supernatural encounter couldn't remedy the issue. Only pastors carrying the heart of God could solve this dilemma. Jesus' heart was to see pastors positioned to love and minister to the sheep of God. We still need this today. Pastors who are called of God. The compassion of Jesus is still crying for this today. It seems everyone would rather be an apostle, prophet, evangelist, or teacher. Nobody seems to desire the place of pastor. Yet Jesus is still moved with the state of His sheep that are scattered and weary. Perhaps if the glory of God could come, from this place and encounter true pastors after the heart of God could be placed. The result of the glory wouldn't be to vibrate, have a vision of angels, or some other heavenly visitation. The result would be to carry the compassion of Jesus for His sheep. This is what the glory produces as well.

Matthew 14:14 also tells us that compassion was the motivating factor in Jesus' healing ministry.

> *And when Jesus went out He saw a great multitude; and He was moved with compassion for them, and healed their sick.*

Jesus' healing of the sick wasn't so He could make a name for Himself. In fact, He would heal the sick and tell them to tell no one. Matthew 8:3-4 shows Jesus not using the healing ministry as a tool to make people think He was awesome.

> *Then Jesus put out His hand and touched him, saying,*

"I am willing; be cleansed."
Immediately his leprosy was
cleansed.

And Jesus said to him, "See
that you tell no one; but go your
way, show yourself to the priest,
and offer the gift that Moses
commanded, as a testimony to
them."

Jesus healed the sick because of His compassion toward them and their need. The
sad truth for many if not most of us is we
want people to get healed so we can become
famous. Oh, we claim it's so Jesus can be
glorified. I'm sure that part is mixed in
somewhere. Yet Jesus healed people because
His great heart of love and compassion compelled Him to. Maybe if this became the

overwhelming reason why we prayed and cried to God, we might see more and greater miracles. May the compassion of Jesus fill our hearts as we encounter His glory. It will change everything. The healing ministry will not be used to manipulate us toward fame, but rather because it flows from a deep sense of His compassion for people.

Jesus also cast demons out because of His compassion. In Mark 5 we find Jesus casting a legion of demons out of a man. This man had been controlled and possessed by demons for years. He was beyond help. That is, until he met Jesus. As Jesus set him free, this man then wanted to go with Jesus. However, in Mark 5:19-20 Jesus tells him to instead to go home and tell family and friends what had happened to him. Notice

Jesus tells him to report to them that the Lord had *compassion* on him.

> *However, Jesus did not permit him, but said to him, "Go home to your friends, and tell them what great things the Lord has done for you, and how He has had compassion on you." And he departed and began to proclaim in Decapolis all that Jesus had done for him; and all marveled.*

It was the compassion of Jesus that set this man free from demonic control. Just like with healing, deliverance should be a result of the great compassion of the Lord moving through us.

I have been one who has yelled at demons in times past. However, I remember one specific situation when a young man was possessed with demons. There were those who were holding him down and calling the demons out. Nothing good was happening in this situation. I told them to let him go. I then drew him close to me and hugged him under my arm. As I held him there and just loved him, over the process of about fifteen minutes three demons left him and he was freed. As I held him close, he would say to me, "A demon just left." No one yelled, bound, or loosed; I just held him in compassion. The result was that complete freedom came to him.

There is great power in the compassion of the Lord. Notice that Jesus told this man to go and tell family and friends what happened to him. However, it says he proclaimed it in the Decapolis. Decapolis was a ten-city region. The compassion of the Lord had so freed him that he went way past what Jesus had told him to do. Jesus said just go home and speak to those who know you. However, driven by the love and compassion of Jesus, he told ten cities of the love and kindness of the Lord. This is His compassion and the power of it. When we are touched by His glory, this compassion can fill us as well.

CHAPTER 7

DIRECTION FOR LIFE

The final thing that God told Moses He would show him when His glory passed him by was direction and guidance for life. We all need to be led by the Lord so that we might follow Him. Yet sometimes it seems that God's will and plan for us is a mystery. This can be because we haven't encountered the glory of the Lord. Within the glory of God is the direction we all crave and yearn for. God told Moses He would put him in the cleft of the rock. He would pass by him. As the face of God passed by, God would cover Moses so that he wouldn't see the face of God. Then He would take His hand away. He would allow Moses to see God's back.

I am told that this, among other things, meant that Moses would have guidance from the Lord. If we stand *behind* someone and watch where they are going, we can tell the direction they are taking. From behind we can discern their movement and the turns they make. When God allows Moses to see His back, He is telling Him, *"I will*

*allow you to discern My movements and the
way I am going. This will permit you to follow with clarity."* This is what God told the
children of Israel when they were prepar-
ing to cross the Jordan River. Joshua 3:3-4
shows that they had to walk behind the Ark
of the Covenant that the priests were carrying. This was so they could see which way
they were heading and follow.

> *And they commanded the people,
> saying, "When you see the ark
> of the covenant of the Lord your
> God, and the priests, the Levites,
> bearing it, then you shall set out
> from your place and go after it.
> Yet there shall be a space between
> you and it, about two thousand
> cubits by measure. Do not come*

near it, that you may know the
way by which you must go, for you
have not passed this way before."

Notice that they were to *go after it*.
This implies they were to pursue. This is
another thing concerning watching from
behind. It requires us to pursue the Lord
as He moves ahead of us. It requires us to
chase after Him with all our hearts. This
reveals a passion in our hearts for the Lord
and His presence and purpose. The glory
of the Lord will create within us a hunger
and thirst for Him. This hunger and thirst
is not a part of natural humanity. In fact,
natural humanity is at enmity with God.
Romans 8:7 is one of several places where
we see that in our human state we don't
desire God.

Because the carnal mind is enmity against God; for it is not subject to the law of God, nor indeed can be.

Enmity with God means we are hostile toward Him. However, when we have been saved, born again, and redeemed, this changes. What we used to hate we now love, and what we used to love we now hate. We have received a new nature like God's. With this new nature comes a thirst for Him. It makes us want to pursue Him in all His ways. This is why we are to stand *behind* Him. We are positioned to pursue after Him from that which has been formed in us by God. *"We love Him because He first loved us"* (I John 4:19).

As the Ark proceeded, they were to stay back a certain distance in their pursuit. This was so they could clearly watch and make the right turns should God move in a given direction. This was because they *"had not passed this way before."* When we see the glory of God it can unlock for us this whole area of discerning the direction of the Lord. We can pursue Him and make the right turns. Following the Lord's leadership can seem difficult as human beings. Yet when we function in and from the glory of God it becomes much easier. We become more sensitive to the Holy Spirit. We no longer are being ruled by the dictates of our flesh but by the Spirit of the Lord. In fact, we are told in Galatians 5:16 that when we walk in the Spirit in agreement with God, we will not allow the flesh to overwhelm us.

*I say then: Walk in the Spirit,
and you shall not fulfill the lust
of the flesh.*

Walking in the Spirit is standing behind the Lord as He moves and following as closely as we can. From this glorious place in the Spirit we can discern His twists and turns and follow without fear but in confidence. The glory of God visited and encountered allows this to happen. We can move with assurance that we are following the Lord into the future that He has for us. His future is glorious and beyond compare. The scripture declares in First Corinthians 2:9-10 that what God has planned we can't imagine.

*But as it is written:
"Eye has not seen, nor ear heard,*

*Nor have entered into the heart
of man*

*The things which God has
prepared for those who love Him."
But God has revealed them to us
through His Spirit. For the Spirit
searches all things, yes, the deep
things of God.*

The Holy Spirit, as He leads us into
the deep place of God's glory, helps us
enter these unimaginable places in God.
Nothing will be withheld from us. All are
available. We simply should cry to God as
Moses did and say, *"Show me Your glory."*
It is His delight to engage us in these
realms. We will be directed by His Holy
Spirit into the unfathomable regions of
His glory and grace. May we encounter His

glory and follow Him closely into His ways
and directions.

ABOUT ROBERT HENDERSON

Robert Henderson is a global apostolic leader who operates in revelation and impartation. His teaching empowers the Body of Christ to see the hidden truths of Scripture clearly and apply them for breakthrough results. Driven by a mandate to disciple nations through writing and speaking, and other forms of media including his show *The Courts of Heaven with Robert Henderson* on GODTV. Robert travels extensively around the globe, teaching on the apostolic, the Kingdom of God, the "Seven Mountains," and, most notably, the Courts of Heaven. He has been married to Mary for over 40 years. They have six children and a growing number of grandchildren. Together they are enjoying life in beautiful Waco, Texas.